D1067960

*This book was a gift
to our library
from Capstone Press.*

The Klondike Gold Rush

by Marc Tyler Nobleman

Content Adviser: Nicolette Bromberg,
Visual Materials Curator, Special Collections,
University of Washington Libraries

Reading Adviser: Rosemary G. Palmer, Ph.D.,
Department of Literacy, College of Education,
Boise State University

COMPASS POINT BOOKS
MINNEAPOLIS, MINNESOTA

Compass Point Books
3109 West 50th Street, #115
Minneapolis, MN 55410

Visit Compass Point Books on the Internet at *www.compasspointbooks.com*
or e-mail your request to *custserv@compasspointbooks.com*

On the cover: Klondike gold miners in the late 1890s use a gold pan and sluice.

Photographs ©: University of Washington Libraries, Special Collections Division, neg. #UW7326, cover; Prints Old & Rare, back cover (far left); Library of Congress, back cover; North Wind Picture Archives, 5; The Granger Collection, New York, 7, 16; Yukon Archives, Glenbow Museum Collection, #2426, 8; Michael DeYoung/Corbis, 10; University of Washington Libraries, Special Collections Division, neg. #Hegg859, 12; University of Washington Libraries, Special Collections Division, neg. #Hegg2159a, 13; University of Washington Libraries, Special Collections Division, neg. #A.Curtis62086, 14; Canada Post Corporation (1996), reproduced with permission, 15; Yukon Archives, James Albert Johnson Collection, 82/341 #21, 17; University of Washington Libraries, Special Collections Division, neg. #UW1830, 18; University of Washington Libraries, Special Collections Division, neg. #W&S4712, 19; Buddy Mays/Corbis, 20; Hulton Archive/Getty Images, 21; Museum of History and Industry/Corbis, 22; University of Washington Libraries, Special Collections Division, neg. #UW4770, 23; University of Washington Libraries, 24; University of Washington Libraries, Special Collections Division, neg. #UW2698, 25; University of Washington Libraries, Special Collections Division, neg. #Hegg97, 27; University of Washington Libraries, Special Collections Division, neg. #Hegg120, 28; University of Washington Libraries, Special Collections Division, neg. #Hegg79, 30; Jack Fields/Corbis, 32; University of Washington Libraries, Special Collections Division, neg. #Hegg208, 33; University of Washington Libraries, Special Collections Division, neg. #Hegg73a, 34; Museum of History & Industry, Seattle, 35; University of Washington Libraries, Special Collections Division, neg. #Hegg29, 36; University of Washington Libraries, Special Collections Division, neg. #A.Curtis46068, 38; University of Washington Libraries, Special Collections Division, neg. #Hegg1167, 39; Bettmann/Corbis, 40.

Managing Editor: Catherine Neitge
Page Production: James Mackey
Photo Researchers: Bobbie Nuytten and Svetlana Zhurkin
Cartographer: XNR Productions, Inc.
Library Consultant: Kathleen Baxter

Creative Director: Keith Griffin
Editorial Director: Carol Jones

Library of Congress Cataloging-in-Publication Data
Nobleman, Marc Tyler.
  The Klondike gold rush / by Marc Tyler Nobleman.
    p. cm. — (We the people)
  Includes bibliographical references and index.
  ISBN 0-7565-1630-7 (hardcover)
  1. Klondike River Valley (Yukon)—Gold discoveries—Juvenile literature. I. Title. II. We the people (Series) (Compass Point Books)
  F1095.K5N63 2006
  971.9'101—dc22   2005025082

TABLE OF CONTENTS

From Newlyweds to Newly Rich 4

Searching for Family and Fortune 10

Birth of a Gold Rush 14

The World Finds Out 19

Preparing to Prospect 23

The Routes to Riches 26

Tough Times on the Trails 32

From Gold to Dust 38

Glossary 42

Did You Know? 43

Important Dates 44

Important People 45

Want to Know More? 46

Index 48

FROM NEWLYWEDS TO NEWLY RICH

In 1896, Ethel and Clarence Berry set out on their honeymoon. Many newlyweds prefer tropical climates. But the Berrys could not afford to go somewhere like that. Instead, they left San Francisco, California, and went north to the Yukon Territory. This northwestern region of Canada on the Alaska border was a remote and wild place.

Ethel and Clarence crossed the treacherous Chilkoot Pass. They prepared to spend the winter in the Klondike region of the Yukon, specifically in a 12-foot-by-16-foot (3.6-meter-by-4.8-meter) wood cabin in the village of Fortymile. "When I got there, the house had no door, windows, or floor," Ethel said, "and I had to stand around outside until a hole was cut for me to get in. We had all the camp-made furniture we needed: a bed and stove." They cut a window in the cabin and covered it with a flour sack. But the sack could not keep out the frigid air.

Gold seekers faced a strenuous climb to the summit of Chilkoot Pass.

Ethel took care of the cabin and cooked, while Clarence prospected for gold in the many tributaries of the Klondike River. Several thousand miners lived in the area. Some had discovered a little gold in the Yukon, but many more searched and found nothing. The common method of looking for gold was placer (pronounced PLASS-er) mining, or panning for gold. Miners placed sand or gravel in a pan and poured water on it to separate any gold flakes from the sediment. Having no luck, Clarence took a job in Fortymile tending bar at a saloon where prospectors were regular customers.

One night, a man came into the saloon and bragged that he had found gold at Rabbit Creek. Clarence quickly headed to the area and staked a claim on nearby Eldorado Creek. The stream was named after El Dorado, the legendary South American city that was supposedly brimming with gold.

For the Berrys, Eldorado Creek was aptly named. They mined for gold through the winter of 1896–1897.

Miners pan for gold in the Klondike in the 1890s.

In July, they returned to San Francisco with other miners aboard the steamship *Excelsior.* Despite her dirty, ragged appearance, Ethel looked cheerful as she stepped off the ship. Her bedroll was too heavy to lift, but not because she

*Ethel Berry and her sister Tot Bush panned for gold in Eldorado Creek while
Clarence Berry shoveled black sand and gold out of the sluice box.*

was tired. It was packed with more than $100,000 worth of gold. She was literally filthy rich.

Ethel became known as the "Bride of the Klondike" and Clarence as the "Luckiest Man in the Klondike"—because of his gold discovery and his wife, who stood beside him when times were tough. They planned to save some of their money, invest some, go back to mine more—and take a "real" honeymoon.

Newspapers published stories of the Berrys and other miners who worked hard and got rich in less than a year. Almost immediately, other people wanted to take the same risk. Thousands dropped everything and left the lives they knew to hunt for Klondike gold.

SEARCHING FOR FAMILY AND FORTUNE

Skookum Jim Mason was worried about his sister. She and her husband had gone into the vast Yukon wilderness in 1889 to look for gold. Skookum Jim hadn't heard from them in seven years. He decided to look for Shaaw Tláa and her husband, George Washington Carmack.

The northern lights flash across the Canadian wilderness.

Skookum Jim and Shaaw Tláa were Native American members of the Tagish nation. Carmack was a white American prospector who had hunted, fished, and prospected with Skookum Jim. When Shaaw Tláa married Carmack, she took the name Kate.

The Carmacks had left the southern Yukon to look for gold in the Fortymile region, about 300 miles (480 kilometers) north. When Skookum Jim set out to find his sister and brother-in-law, two of his nephews accompanied him, Tagish Charlie (later called Dawson Charlie) and Patsy Henderson. The three men found George and Kate camped at the mouth of the Klondike River, where they were fishing for salmon.

George reportedly told them that he had dreamed of salmon with gold nuggets for eyes. Shortly after, he, Skookum Jim, and Tagish Charlie went moose hunting a few miles up the Klondike River. They encountered another prospector, Robert Henderson (no relation to Patsy). Henderson would have allowed George to help him search for gold on his claim, but he didn't want the other two around because they were Indians. So the three men moved on, possibly taking Henderson's suggestion about where to explore instead.

Prospectors, including Skookum Jim Mason (second from right) and Tagish Charlie (far right), pose on the porch of a Klondike cabin in the late 1890s.

12

Skookum Jim (center) with other prospectors at his Rabbit Creek claim

They discovered a small tributary of the Klondike River called Rabbit Creek—and it was there on August 16, 1896, that George, Skookum Jim, and Tagish Charlie discovered gold. As someone of the era might have said, they hit pay dirt. And it appeared to be more gold than anyone had previously found on one site in the Yukon.

If George did indeed have a vision of gold, it had come true.

13

BIRTH OF A GOLD RUSH

George Carmack is frequently credited as being the one who discovered the gold. According to one story, he saw a thumb-sized nugget sticking out from the bank of the creek. Yet some historians believe that Skookum Jim came across the gold. According to that story, Skookum Jim went to the creek for a drink and saw gold flakes glimmering between stones in the water like "cheese in a sandwich." The men dipped a pan into the gravel and came up with more than ¼ ounce (7 grams) of gold.

In any event, the one

George Washington Carmack

14

Skookum Jim Mason's image appeared on a Canadian postage stamp in 1996, the 100th anniversary of the Klondike gold strike.

who staked the first official claim was George Carmack. Skookum Jim and Tagish Charlie didn't because white miners might not respect a claim made by a Native American. But the two men staked a smaller claim along-side George's claim. The three agreed to share the mining work—and the profits.

Robert Henderson, however, was out of luck. It was

15

customary for a miner who found gold because of another miner's tip to let that miner know. But because Henderson had not been tolerant of his Indian family members, Carmack didn't tell him about the riches of Rabbit Creek.

Carmack hurried to Fortymile to record his discovery. He popped into a popular saloon and said, "Boys, there's been a strike on Rabbit Creek." Clarence Berry was

Gold seekers forded the Dyea River on their way to the Klondike.

one of the "boys" who heard the announcement.

Some prospectors had trouble believing Carmack since he had a reputation for lying. But they couldn't dispute the evidence. Most people in the Klondike had "gold fever" and would not let opportunities pass them by.

Word of the discovery traveled fast throughout the Yukon River valley. Within

Kate Carmack wore a necklace made from gold nuggets.

two weeks, hundreds of prospectors had stampeded to the Klondike. Appropriately, they were soon called stampeders. Prospectors who found gold were dubbed "Klondike kings."

Many staked claims on Rabbit Creek, which was renamed Bonanza Creek. Others staked claims on nearby

17

A prospector and his puppy Yukon on Eldorado Creek in 1897

streams, such as Eldorado Creek. Henderson showed up eventually, but he was too late. Others had already staked all the desirable land.

Before the Klondike discovery, miners were happy if they found 4 or 5 cents' worth of gold in one pan. Now many were finding several hundred dollars in one pan. George and Kate Carmack, Skookum Jim, and Tagish Charlie made about $1 million on their claim.

The Klondike gold rush was on. No one knew yet, but it would be the biggest and last of the great northern gold rushes.

THE WORLD FINDS OUT

By the end of 1896, approximately 3,000 Yukoners had flocked to the Klondike to search for gold. The outside world, however, still did not know what was happening. The Yukon River froze in late September, and the winter was harsh. This limited communication in and out.

That changed in July 1897 when two steamships loaded with jubilant Klondike miners and their gold pulled into two American harbors. The *Excelsior* docked in San Francisco, and the *Portland* docked in Seattle. An estimated $500,000 of gold was onboard the *Excelsior.* The *Portland* had $1 million. About 5,000 people

Crowds in Seattle awaited the arrival of steamships from the gold fields in 1897.

19

welcomed the *Portland* miners. "Show us the gold!" they shouted, and the miners obliged by holding up full bags. Some miners threw gold nuggets to the crowd.

The spectators cheered as if the miners were royalty. Yet in most cases, their fortunes wouldn't last long. The majority of miners would soon spend most of their earnings without saving or investing much.

But for the moment, all was glorious. Newspapers told the miners' stories. A headline in the *Seattle Post-*

Gold nuggets lie in a pan of water

20

A group of miners at a Bonanza Creek claim in 1897

Intelligencer screamed "Gold, Gold, Gold!" The Klondike
gold rush was probably the most publicized gold rush of
its time. Since 1893, the United States had been suffering
through an economic depression in which many people lost
their jobs. Some thought the Klondike could solve their
financial problems. Some heard that miners were return-
ing to the United States with *crates* of gold. They wanted a
piece of the wealth.

21

Gold seekers crowded a Seattle wharf seeking passage to the Klondike.

The Klondike gold rush was on—again. Tens of thousands of people planned trips there as fast as they could. Most had no idea how difficult the journey would be. None knew that local prospectors had taken most of the valuable claims.

Even though they thought the gold rush was just starting, it was actually over. Still, they had quite an adventure ahead of them.

PREPARING TO PROSPECT

Various American and Canadian cities in the Northwest began to compete with each other for the business that the gold rush would generate. San Francisco, California; Seattle and Tacoma, Washington; Astoria and Portland, Oregon; and Victoria and Vancouver, British Columbia, all wanted to be the "official" stopover city for prospectors on their way to the Klondike.

The people looking for gold would need outfits, or prospecting and mining supplies. City governments knew that could mean big business. A typical outfit included dried fruit and smoked bacon, clothing, camping gear, medical supplies, and tools—and cost between $250 and $700.

A Seattle store sold outfits, or supplies, to prospectors heading north.

23

Seattle Chamber of Commerce advertisement

Because of Erastus Brainerd, Seattle won the competition. Brainerd was the head of a committee called the Bureau of Information, which was formed by the Seattle Chamber of Commerce. Its goal was to promote Seattle to stampeders. Brainerd placed advertisements in periodicals nationwide. He sent a special Klondike edition of the *Seattle Post-Intelligencer* newspaper to more than 100,000 post offices, libraries, newspaper editors, and railways. He even wrote personal letters to the rulers and embassies of foreign governments, inviting them to come.

His efforts paid off. Brainerd alone was a major reason the Klondike gold rush grew as large as it did. In the process, Seattle grew considerably, too. Its population nearly doubled in the 1890s.

It wasn't just city governments that took advantage of the gold rush crowds. Since few prospectors were familiar with the region, a number of companies published guide-

Erastus Brainerd went to the Yukon, but like most others, did not strike it rich.

books to assist them. Some of the guidebooks were helpful, but many were useless. Often their "facts" were intentional lies—for example, a claim that everyone who looked for gold would find some.

THE ROUTES TO RICHES

The Klondike was far north in Canada, about 2,000 miles (3,200 km) from Seattle. Prospectors had a choice of many routes to get there. One was the "rich man's route." It was a 4,000-mile (6,400-km) steamship trip on the Pacific Ocean and the Bering Sea, then through Alaska on the Yukon River. Ice blocked this route most of the year.

Of the many land routes, two became the most widely traveled. An estimated 90 percent of stampeders took either White Pass or Chilkoot Pass. Both paths started in Alaskan port towns and both required a grueling mountain hike and a 500-mile (800-km) boat ride down the Yukon River.

The White Pass route began in Skagway. The Chilkoot Pass route, named for the Chilkoot Indians who used it for centuries, began in Dyea. Travelers took a ship to get to either of these towns. They were 3 miles (4.8 km) apart and about 600 miles (960 km) south of the goldfields.

Gold seekers climbed single file up Chilkoot Pass.

Miners crossed a log bridge on the White Pass trail.

Like the big port cities to the south, these two small towns competed for miners. As miners came, so did new businesses. Yet both remained "Wild West" towns, where conmen thrived and law enforcement was nearly nonexistent.

White Pass was a 45-mile (72-km) rocky, muddy trail. As it zigzagged higher, it narrowed to 2 feet (60 centimeters) across, and ran along a cliff that dropped hundreds

28

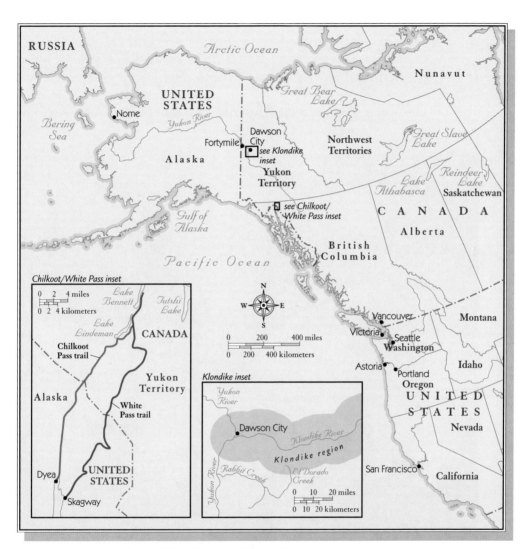

Most prospectors took the White Pass or Chilkoot Pass.

of feet. Between 5,000 and 10,000 people took this route

during the winter of 1897–1898. But the White Pass trail

was too strenuous for pack animals. More than 3,000 horses

29

died along it, and some of their bones are still there today. It became known as the Dead Horse Trail.

Chilkoot Pass was a 32-mile (51-km) trail between

The approach to Chilkoot Pass following an April 1898 avalanche

coastal mountains. Even though it was shorter than White Pass, it was considered more demanding. It earned the nickname "the meanest 32 miles in the world." Pack animals couldn't continue on near the end of the trail. The final stretch of Chilkoot Pass, called the "golden stairs," had 1,500 steps cut into snow and ice. The last 1,000 feet (305 m) stretched almost straight up. The steps were so narrow that stampeders climbed them single file. It could take six hours to reach the top.

Between 25,000 and 30,000 people took the Chilkoot trail during the winter and spring of 1897–1898. On April 3, 1898, when the gold rush was in its most frenzied stage, an avalanche pounded down Chilkoot Pass. It dumped snow as deep as 30 feet (9 m) and killed more than 60 people.

TOUGH TIMES ON THE TRAILS

Travel on the trails was exhausting, no matter the season. Winter temperatures could reach 70 below zero (57 below zero Celsius), and snowstorms were fierce. Summer brought fog and rain, which made the steep ground slippery. Some people crawled, rather than walked, over boulders. Murder, suicide, disease, and accidents also plagued some of the stampeders on the trails. Many turned back. It often took more than three months to get to the Klondike. These travelers were warned that no matter which trail they chose, they'd soon wish they'd chosen the other.

A grave marker bears the name of a miner who died on Chilkoot Pass.

32

Miners with their tons of gear rested on the summit of Chilkoot Pass in 1898.

Adding to the stampeders' exhaustion was the amount of gear they had to bring. The Northwest Mounted Police, sometimes called the Mounties, required each stampeder to take a year's supply of necessities into the Yukon. That worked out to about a ton of supplies! This was to prevent shortages and starvation since there were few, if any, places along the way to purchase supplies.

33

Stampeders couldn't move all that weight at once. Their goods were divided into 50-pound (22.5-kilogram) packs. They moved one pack of goods up the trail, then went back down for another pack. They went back and forth on the same section of the trail until they slowly moved their whole ton of supplies forward. One trip up the mountain was actually 40 trips.

Some stampeders lugged their supplies on their backs or on sleds. Some hired Indians or college students to carry their supplies. In late 1897 and early 1898, aerial tramways were built next to the stairs of the Chilkoot Pass. Construction of

Klondike miners hauled their supplies on horse-drawn sleds.

a railway on the White Pass began in 1898. But both were too late for stampeders. The White Pass & Yukon Railroad secured the survival of Skagway, where it began, and led to the end of Dyea.

Once the stampeders made it over the trails, they reached either Lake Bennett or Lake Lindeman. There they cut trees and built boats for the next part of the trek:

After leaving the lakes, stampeders faced treacherous rapids on the Yukon River.

the Yukon River. The lakes were near the timberline, so finding trees was a problem. The stampeders used what trees there were until eventually the surrounding forest

Supplies arrived in Dawson City by pack train in the late 1890s.

was almost bare. Once their boats were finished, they waited. When the spring thaw came at the end of May, about 7,000 boats got on the river. It was a rough ride, and more than 100 boats didn't make it.

Three weeks later, their journey ended at Dawson City, the last stop before the goldfields. Dawson City was built for the sudden mob of prospectors. Between 1896 and 1898, the town's population swelled from zero to more than 30,000. But after months of backbreaking effort to get there, stampeders arrived in the summer of 1898 only to learn that other miners had already staked all the good creeks—almost a year earlier.

FROM GOLD TO DUST

When the stampeders found out there was no longer any promising place to look for gold, they were unsure of what to do. Some turned around and went home. Others stayed

Disappointed gold seekers sold their outfits along the Dawson City waterfront in 1898.

38

in Dawson City and worked on someone else's claim or at a local business.

In 1899, word reached the town that prospectors had struck gold in Nome, Alaska. Many stampeders left the Klondike to try again farther west. By 1901, the population of Dawson City had dwindled to 9,000.

About 100,000 people had tried to make it to the Klondike. About 40,000 succeeded, and about half of that number actually mined for gold. Only about 4,000 of those found gold. And that

A gold miner and his dogs outside his Nome, Alaska, cabin in 1900

Miners sought their fortune and adventure in the Klondike gold rush.

didn't make them all instantly rich. It depended on the amount they found—and on how much money they'd spent to get there. Many of the rest returned home dusty and poor.

But they lived through what many call the last grand adventure of the 19th century. They didn't get rich, but they made history just the same. They were part of the great Klondike gold rush.

GLOSSARY

bedroll—bedding rolled up for carrying

bonanza—a very large, rich mineral deposit

pay dirt—ore that is profitable

placer mining—a type of mining in which loose fragments of valuable ore are separated from the surrounding sand or gravel, as in panning for gold

sediment—small rocks, dirt, and other matter carried and left by water

staked a claim—reserved a section of public land on which to look for gold

timberline—the point on mountainsides beyond which trees do not grow

tramways—transportation systems for moving minerals or people; some are on the ground and some are in the air

tributaries—streams that flow into larger streams or rivers

DID YOU KNOW?

- Stampeders were not all men. Women came to the Klondike to mine, open shops, run restaurants and hotels, report for newspapers, work in libraries, and perform in dance halls. Some came with their husbands, while others were on their own.

- Mail delivery was a challenge in the Klondike. Mail carriers had the same obstacles traveling through the region that the stampeders did. Plus the stampeders moved around and could be hard to find. In almost all of their correspondence, stampeders complained that they weren't getting enough letters from home.

- The Northwest Mounted Police kept peace and order in the Canadian Yukon during the Klondike gold rush. By comparison, Alaskan towns such as Skagway and Dyea had little law enforcement and were overrun with crime.

- A young man named Jack London was a witness to the Klondike gold rush. He crossed Chilkoot Pass in the winter of 1897–1898 with 22,000 other stampeders. London wrote stories and books based on his experience. Two of his popular books are *The Call of the Wild* (1903) and *White Fang* (1906).

IMPORTANT DATES

Timeline

1896	In August, George Carmack, Skookum Jim Mason, and Tagish Charlie discover gold in Rabbit Creek, a tributary of the Klondike River in the Yukon Territory.
1896– 1897	Local miners find millions of dollars worth of gold in the Klondike in winter.
1897	Miners return to San Francisco and Seattle on July 14 and July 17 with news of—and bags of—gold; stampeders from across the country and around the world set out in summer to search for gold in the Klondike.
1898	Thousands more prospectors head to the Klondike in the spring; an avalanche at the Chilkoot Pass on April 3 kills more than 60 people; as many as 30,000 prospectors arrive in Dawson City in the summer, but they're too late: The gold claims are already taken.
1899	Miners rush to Nome, Alaska, in the spring when word reaches Dawson City of a gold strike there.

IMPORTANT PEOPLE

CLARENCE BERRY (c. 1867–1930)
AND ETHEL BERRY (1873–1948)
Newlyweds who first struck gold in the Klondike in 1896 and built on their wealth throughout their lives

ERASTUS BRAINERD (1855–1922)
Promoter whose marketing campaign at the beginning of the Klondike gold rush transformed Seattle, Washington, into a major city

GEORGE CARMACK (1850–1922)
AND KATE CARMACK (1867–1920)
American prospector and his Tagish wife (also known as Shaaw Tláa) who discovered gold in a tributary of the Klondike River in 1896, which led to the Klondike gold rush; several years later, Carmack abandoned his wife, who received nothing from the gold claims

SKOOKUM JIM MASON (c. 1855–1916)
Tagish Indian and brother of Shaaw Tláa (Kate Carmack) who discovered gold in a tributary of the Klondike River in 1896, which led to the Klondike gold rush; his Tagish name was Keish and he left a large amount of his wealth to benefit Yukon native people

WANT TO KNOW MORE?

At the Library

Cooper, Michael. *Klondike Fever: The Famous Gold Rush of 1898.* New York: Clarion Books, 1989.

Murphy, Claire Rudolf, and Jane G. Haigh. *Children of the Gold Rush.* Portland, Ore.: Alaska Northwest Books, 2001.

Shepherd, Donna Walsh. *The Klondike Gold Rush.* New York: Franklin Watts, 1998.

On the Web

For more information on the *Klondike Gold Rush*, use FactHound to track down Web sites related to this book.

1. Go to *www.facthound.com*
2. Type in a search word related to this book or this book ID: 0756516307
3. Click on the *Fetch It* button.

Your trusty FactHound will fetch the best Web sites for you!

On the Road

Klondike Gold Rush National Historical Park
Second and Broadway
Box 517
Skagway, AK 99840
907/983-2921
Fifteen restored buildings in the Skagway historic district

Klondike Gold Rush National Historical Park
Seattle Visitor Center
117 S. Main St.
Seattle, WA 98104
206/553-7220
Gold-panning demonstrations, exhibits, programs, and tours

Look for more We the People books about this era:

The Alamo
ISBN 0-7565-0097-4

The Arapaho and Their History
ISBN 0-7565-0831-2

The Battle of the Little Bighorn
ISBN 0-7565-0150-4

The Buffalo Soldiers
ISBN 0-7565-0833-9

The California Gold Rush
ISBN 0-7565-0041-9

California Ranchos
ISBN 0-7565-1633-1

The Cherokee and Their History
ISBN 0-7565-1273-5

The Chumash and Their History
ISBN 0-7565-0835-5

The Creek and Their History
ISBN 0-7565-0836-3

The Erie Canal
ISBN 0-7565-0679-4

Great Women of Pioneer America
ISBN 0-7565-1269-7

Great Women of the Old West
ISBN 0-7565-0099-0

The Iroquois and Their History
ISBN 0-7565-1272-7

The Lewis and Clark Expedition
ISBN 0-7565-0044-3

The Library of Congress
ISBN 0-7565-1631-5

The Louisiana Purchase
ISBN 0-7565-0210-1

The Mexican War
ISBN 0-7565-0841-X

The Ojibwe and Their History
ISBN 0-7565-0843-6

The Oregon Trail
ISBN 0-7565-0045-1

The Pony Express
ISBN 0-7565-0301-9

The Powhatan and Their History
ISBN 0-7565-0844-4

The Pueblo and Their History
ISBN 0-7565-1274-3

The Santa Fe Trail
ISBN 0-7565-0047-8

The Sioux and Their History
ISBN 0-7565-1275-1

The Trail of Tears
ISBN 0-7565-0101-6

The Transcontinental Railroad
ISBN 0-7565-0153-9

The Wampanoag and Their History
ISBN 0-7565-0847-9

The War of 1812
ISBN 0-7565-0848-7

The Wilderness Road
ISBN 0-7565-1637-4

A complete list of We the People titles is available on our Web site:
www.compasspointbooks.com

INDEX

Astoria, Oregon, 23
avalanches, 31

Berry, Clarence, 4, 6–9, 16
Berry, Ethel, 4, 6–9
boats, 35–37
Bonanza Creek, 17
Brainerd, Erastus, 24–25
Bureau of Information, 24

cabins, 4
Carmack, George Washington, 10, 11–13, 14, 15, 16, 17, 18
Carmack, Shaaw Tláa "Kate," 10–11, 18
Chilkoot Indians, 26
Chilkoot Pass, 4, 26, 30–31, 34
claims, 6, 12, 15, 17–18, 22, 37, 39

Dawson City, 37, 39
Dead Horse Trail, 30
Dyea, 26, 28, 35

Eldorado Creek, 6, 18
Excelsior (steamship), 7, 19

Fortymile, 4, 6, 11, 16

gold, 6, 8, 9, 13, 14, 18, 19, 20, 21, 39, 41
guidebooks, 25

Henderson, Patsy, 11
Henderson, Robert, 11–12, 15–16, 18

"Klondike kings," 17
Klondike River, 6, 11, 13

Lake Bennett, 35–36
Lake Lindeman, 35–36

map of Klondike, 29
Mason, Skookum Jim, 10–11, 11–13, 14, 15, 18
Mounties. *See* Northwest Mounted Police.

Nome, Alaska, 39
Northwest Mounted Police, 33

outfits, 23, 34

placer mining, 6
Portland (steamship), 19–20
Portland, Oregon, 23
publicity, 20–21, 24–25

Rabbit Creek, 6, 13, 16, 17
railways, 35

San Francisco, California, 4, 7, 19, 23
Seattle Chamber of Commerce, 24
Seattle Post-Intelligencer (newspaper), 20–21, 24
Seattle, Washington, 19, 23, 24, 25
Skagway, 26, 28, 35
stampeders, 17, 24, 26, 31, 32, 33–34, 35, 36–37, 38–39, 41
steamships, 7, 19–20, 26
stopover cities, 23
supplies. *See* outfits.

Tacoma, Washington, 23
Tagish Charlie, 11–13, 15, 18
Tagish nation, 11
tramways, 34

Vancouver, British Columbia, 23
Victoria, British Columbia, 23

White Pass, 26, 28–30, 35
White Pass & Yukon Railroad, 35

Yukon River, 17, 19, 26, 36
Yukon Territory, 4

About the Author

Marc Tyler Nobleman is the author of more than 40 books for young people. He writes regularly for *Nickelodeon Magazine* and has written for The History Channel. He is also a cartoonist whose single panels have appeared in more than 100 international publications, including the *Wall Street Journal, Good Housekeeping,* and *Forbes.* He lives with his wife and daughter in Connecticut.